TABLE OF CONTENTS

PART 1: THE BASICS OF MAKING MEDICINAL TEAS

Tea Basics:

Tea is the beverage that has bound people from generation to generation. Across all cultures and time periods, there are teas that are either utilized for recreational and/or medicinal purposes.

Disclaimer:

As a word of warning, none of the teas shown and described in this book are legally or formally FDA approved. Nevertheless, many people still enjoy them and find they obtain medicinal benefits from them. In any case, you should consult your doctor before using these as a form of medicinal therapy. The content shown in this book is not meant to be a replacement or substitution for professional medical advice. While I can't personally guarantee that you will love these teas, I can give you the 100% promise that you will have fun or learn something in the process of reading this book.

Brewing Styles:

Since there are many different herbs and ingredients that can be used in the making of tea, there are many different ways to brew tea. These different methods of brewing can either help you infuse and brew certain ingredients in your tea, or help you create your tea with the temperature/flavor that you prefer.

Hot Infused Tea:

Hot tea infusion is one of the most basic forms of tea steeping. It utilizes heated water (specific to the cup of tea) that has flavor from plant material infused into it. Aromatic leaves, flowers and roots are all ideal ingredients for hot infusions. With a hot infusion, their basic flavor (and how they smell) will be easily infused into the water. Some common examples of plants for tea that can be grown in your backyard garden are mint, lavender, lemon balm, lemon verbena, sage and thyme. In general for green teas you should have water between 170-185 degrees fahrenheit, white for darker herbal and black teas, you should have water between 208-212 degrees fahrenheit. Temperature is very important because without the proper heat, the flavor compounds will not fully dissolve, leaving your tea rather tasteless and bland. This also explains why most "cold" or "iced" teas must start hot, because the common black and herbal teas used must be heated to specific temperatures in order to release their flavor properly

Iced Tea:

For the classic iced tea, you should use either herbal or black tea leaves (although you can experiment with other plants according to your taste preferences). When brewing an iced tea, you normally brew multiple tea bags (or a higher concentration of tea) in a relatively small amount of water. After the tea has brewed to a very strong and concentrated level, you can add water or ice (to your preference) and let it chill on the countertop or in the fridge. This allows the very concentrated tea to chill to a cold temperature, while diluting to a more palatable flavor. Due to its relatively fast brewing time and high concentration, iced tea tends to have more complex and harsh flavors which are more commonly found in herbal and black teas. In addition to this, many people add sugar or other tea additives in order to create many different types of tea, such as southern sweet tea.

Long Brew Cold-Infusion:

This type of tea brewing is most commonly used for medicinal plants, which people want to pull the most compounds out of, without burning or altering the natural flavor and properties of the tea. Long brew cold-infusion brewing is when tea is placed in lukewarm or cold water in order to brew for a long time on the countertop or in the fridge. This allows for the plant to fully infuse as much as possible into the water without scorching or burning the leaves over time. Commonly, people brew this as an overnight tea in a mason jar in their fridge. In addition to this, most people use this method to brew lighter green and herbal teas which in general don't need higher temperatures to steep. This allows for all of the flavor to steep over a long period of time, so as many nutrients and flavor compounds are released as possible. In some cases people also mash and stir up the leaves while brewing, in order to mechanically pull out some flavor, rather than doing it with hot water. Some common materials used in this type of brewing are flowers, light aromatic herbs such as lavender, and the rinds of citrus fruit such as lemons and oranges.

Sun Tea:

This type of brewing is also used for many medicinal plants, similar to the long brew cold-infusion. In this case, people (especially those who live in warmer climates) place water and tea in a sealed container such as a pitcher or mason jar, and leave it to brew in the sun for a long period of time (3-5+ hours). Not only does this allow for the plants to brew for a longer period of time, releasing more healthy compounds, but it allows you to use less power, and prevent overheating in your kitchen during the summer months. Similar to iced teas, most people tend to use black tea or stronger herbal plants to create this infusion.

Brewing Materials:

As shown before, there are countless ways that people brew tea, that are very specific to the plants they use, the environment that they use them in, and their personal preferences. Similarly, depending on how you want your tea to be prepared, the materials you use will differ. In general some of the materials that you will need to make a cup of tea will include:

- A Manual or Electric Tea Kettle for heating water
- A Pot for brewing on the stove with loose leaf teas
- Tea Bags or Tea Strainers for loose leaf teas
- A Dish or Compost bin for used leaves and bags
- A Cup or Mason jar for drinking and brewing
- Ice cubes to cool down or dilute tea
- An airtight container for storing your custom tea blends
- Any tea additives such as vinegar, honey, or sugar

Customizing Blends:

As with everything, people have different taste preferences and materials to make their own tea. In addition to this, some also look for specific medicinal herbs to include in tea to help a certain ailment they may have. Luckily since it is so diverse, anyone can make any custom blend for any use. As a rule of thumb, always remember to start slow with any new custom tea blend, as you may have a negative reaction to any of the ingredients used within it. As a good recommendation, while you start to try teas and make your own, it is good to keep a list of ingredients that you like the taste of and respond to well, while also keeping a list of ingredients that you may negatively react to, or not like the taste of. In addition to this, while you may be trying to drink tea for health purposes, it always helps to keep the tea palatable, as it will be easier to enjoy while reaping the benefits of the natural ingredients. Because of this, it is good to keep in mind which ingredients are a bit more bitter, or harder to attain, as you may want to use those sparingly. For example If you were making a tea to aid in your digestion and wanted to use dandelion root (which is very bitter), you would want to use a small portion of the dandelion root, in comparison to more flavorful plants such as mint and lemon balm.

PART 2: COMMON HERBS USED IN MEDICINAL TEAS:

Mint

Description:

Mint is a highly aromatic plant that produces stems of bright green leaves. Depending on the variety of mint, their leaves tend to be very square. This applies to other plants in the mint family as well, such as lemon balm. The leaves are arranged in pairs directly opposite of each other, and the plant forms root systems consisting of runners that help propagate the plant naturally. This causes mint to be a very hardy plant, often taking over any flower bed or garden plot that you plant it in.

Cultivation and Parts Used:

As long as the soil is kept moist, mint thrives in full sun, but it can also grow in partial shade. In any case, as it sends out runners and grows vigorously, it is considered semi-invasive and should have success in most environments. Typically mint is cut above a node of growth and the leaves are used fresh. In addition, you can also tie a bundle of stems together and hang them to dry in a cool, dark place. After they are fully dry you can store the leaves and use them for up to a year.

Flavor Profile:

Not surprisingly, mint tea tastes rather "minty." In addition, it is mildly sweet to the taste and cools the mouth and body when ingested, similar to eating mint hard candy. Mint also tends to be very light and refreshing, which makes it great to pair in summer drinks with more fruity flavors.

Medicinal Properties:

Mint is known for its properties that aid in digestion. In general many utilize mint's anti-inflammatory properties while they are sick to slow mucous production and open the airways. It has also been used automatically to help relieve headaches. Finally, mint also has shown calming effects, and is made into a bedtime tea by many people.

Lemon Verbena

Description:

Lemon Verbena is a semi-hardy, woody shrub That produces long, sharp green leaves. The leaves produce a strong citrus scent, very similar to fresh lemons. The scent is also very light and refreshing both in taste and smell.

During propagation, the plant produces small White flowers.

Cultivation and Parts Used:

Lemon verbena loves well-drained soil that is
very loose. The plant also loves full sun and
warm temperatures, which makes it a great candidate for potting and
weathering during the winter months. If you are growing multiple plants, it is
best to spread them relatively far apart so they have room to grow bushy.
Typically, people use the leaves fresh from the stem or hang them to dry
similar to mint. Store them in an airtight container for later usage.

Flavor Profile:

Similar to other lemon-based plants, lemon verbena has a light, lemony
flavor. On the other hand, compared to stronger lemon herbs such as lemon
thyme or mint, lemon verbena is far lighter and less aggressive, more similar
to the light scent of a lemon, rather than the taste of one.

Medicinal Properties:

Similar to lemon balm, lemon verbena contains a strong lemon-scented
volatile oil that has very calming properties. This makes it a great herb to
include in a night time tea. In addition to this, lemon verbena also has
soothing properties that help the digestive system. Many people utilize this
herb to help relieve discomfort in the abdominal region. Although its nervous
system properties are weaker than lemon balm, it is also used to lift the spirits
in attempts to help aid with depression.

Lemon Balm

Description:

Lemon Balm is a bushy plant very similar to mint. It also grows in bushy stocks that tend to be fairly hardy. In addition to this, lemon balm has a very strong and sweet lemony smell and flavor. The leaves tend to be broad and oval or heart shaped, with small irregular serrations lining the edges.

Cultivation and Parts Used:

While lemon balm prefers a well-drained soil, it usually tends to thrive in most soil conditions as long as it does not remain soggy. To harvest the lemon balm, you should either pluck the leaves for immediate use, or hang to dry for later storage, similar to how you would prepare mint for later use. In addition, like most mint-like plants, trimming above a leaf node tends to make the plant grow back stronger and more bushy, leaving you more plant material to work with in the future. While the leaves are the major part used in the plant, some people also use the stems, which also hold a strong citrus flavor.

Flavor Profile:

Lemon balm has a strong and rather aggressive lemony taste. In addition to this, it also has subtle hints of mint that can bridge the gap well between fruit and herbal flavors in a homemade tea. Due to the pleasant flavor, people use this both for recreation and it's medicinal properties. In fact, many people use lemon balm in generous amounts to hide some more unpleasant medicinal flavors such as dandelion root.

Medicinal Properties:

Lemon balm holds many medicinal properties, such as the ability to relieve cold sores, calm the mind and soothe emotional headaches. Similar to other plants in the mint family, lemon balm is known for its strong soothing abilities, and its properties that can help aid in digestion. The volatile oil found within lemon balm (citral and citronella) work to calm the nervous system. On top of this the volatile oils are also very antispasmodic.

Chamomile

Description: Chamomile is a plant that has been used for reacreation and medicine since ancient time. It is closely reltaed to the daisy, and its foliage and flowers have a strong perfume-like scent. The plant produces flowers with bright yellow centers and soft white petals.

Cultivation and Parts Used:

Chamomile plants grow best in full sun, however in warmer environments, it is best to keep them in partial shade to avoid burning or scorching. You can hang them to dry similar to mint and other herbs. In general, for medicinal and tea making purposes, we utilize the flowers and the essential oil from the plant (although it is advised to not use the essential oil internally).

Flavor Profile:

Chamomile has a rather floral taste, similar to its perfume-like scent. In addition to this, it has notes of fruits such as apple and orange. It also has a sweet taste, similar to honey that tends to be very smooth, especially when compared to harsher black teas. Due to these flavors, many people drink chamomile for pleasure, also adding it to night time teas for it's soothing flavor and effect on the body.

Medicinal Properties:

Chamomile is known to be a very relaxing herb. It has been used to sooth the muscles of the stomach to ease digestion or abdominal pains. It's calming effects also translate to the nervous system, making it one of the central plants used to make night-time teas. Lastly, roman chamomile has also been used to help with migraines and headaches, and some people also use its oils as a soothing salve for irritated skin.

Sage

Description:

Like many other plants described here, sage is a plant that is found in the mint family. Sage grows like an evergreen shrub with medium, soft leaves. The leaves are seen as greyish-green with a soft texture similar to velvet or cotton. Sage has a fragrant aroma (similar to some green teas) that is strong when released out of the leaves.

Cultivation and Parts Used:

Sage prefers full sun environments. It also prefers a rather well drained soil, although it is fairly hardy. On the other hand, it will not thrive in conditions where it is constantly sitting in wet or moist soil. Similar to most plants in the mint family, you should continuously prune sage to keep it healthy and bushy. Annually, most people tend to cut down to the woody stems after each growing season to winter the plant. To harvest you can pinch off leaves or hang stems to dry, although you should trim sparingly in the first year so that it grows to its full potential.

Flavor Profile:

As previously stated, sage has a taste/smell similar to some green teas. It smells and tastes very herbal and earthy, making it a great pair to have with more lighter, fruity flavors. Most people also agree that sage has a very warm flavor and sensation when ingested as a tea.

Medicinal Properties:

Sage has been used to help aid ailments in the mouth. People often apply it directly to cold sores, sore mouth areas, and areas of gingivitis to help relieve symptoms. Many also claim that it helps soothe an upset stomach, and that it can help with asthma when inhaled in small amounts. Lastly, sage has been shown to help digestion, especially with fattier foods such as duck and cow. This makes it a great herb to use while cooking.

Thyme

Description: Thyme is a low growing, rather bushy herb. It grows in dense, woody stems that are adorned with small leaves. These leaves are small and ovular and are close together in sprigs that give off a very strong scent. The leaves are also a green-gray color and are found throughout the entirety of the stems.

Cultivation and Parts Used:

Like most herbs, thyme likes well drained soil with plenty of sunlight. While you should water thyme on a regular basis, it is rather drought resistant, so you should only water when the soil is thoroughly dry. The best way to multiply your thyme is through propagation (rather than seeds). The scented leaves are the main part of the plant that is used medicinally and recreationally. To use fresh and dry you can pull them off the stem with your hands in one motion.

Flavor Profile:

Thyme sells very similar to other herbs such as oregano. It has a dry smell and taste that is very warm. For this reason, it is often used in many meat dishes such as poultry or soup broths. Many people also find that thyme has light undertones of mint as well.

Medicinal Properties:

Thyme's main properties relate to the digestive and the respiratory system. Most notably, thyme is heavily used for ailments involving the respiratory system. Many drink it in tea or inhale its diffused essential oils in order to help with different respiratory illnesses such as asthma. In addition to this, thyme is antibacterial and has been used to kill germs, especially in products such as mouthwash to fight bad breath (caused by germs and bacteria).

Lemongrass

Description:

Lemon grass is actually a perennial grass, and it is found in the poaceae family. It grows fragrant leaves and stocks which are often used in cooking. The grass tends to grow in very dense clumps with blades of long grass that droop at the ends. The grass also tends to be a lighter green in color, and is differentiated from other grasses by its large blades of grass.

Cultivation and Parts Used:

Lemongrass likes very well drained soil that is also fairly fertile. Provide the grass with consistent moisture and water at least every time the top inch becomes dry. Lemongrass is also a tropical plant, so it does need a bit of protection from colder weather and temperatures. In general, lemongrass also prefers an environment with full sun.

Flavor Profile:

Lemongrass has a fairly citrus heavy, lemony flavor. In addition to this, it also has a similar flavor to lemon mint (with more earthy tones rather than pure citrus). It has a very light flavor and does not overpower many ingredients, making it great in most dishes and teas,

Medicinal Properties:

Lemongrass is well known for its overall health benefits, making it a fast going fad food to include in many diets and health foods. Lemongrass is also known for its antioxidant properties and its ability to regulate higher blood pressures. It is also a diuretic and helps manage cholesterol levels.

Rooibos

Description:

Rooibos is a bushy plant in the fabaceae family. It grows naturally in South Africa and is a staple type of tea across the world today. People attribute its flavor in tea to that of hibiscus, with a tinge of yerba mate.

Cultivation and Parts Used:

Rooibos prefers to be grown in rather nutrient deficient soil, so don't fertilize anywhere near it. Due to its native habitat, it also prefers to be planted in sandy, loose soil such as soil you would find in a dry, desert environment. Similar to other woody herbs, rooibos is harvested by drying or using the leaves straight off of the woody stocks, which should be pruned regularly.

Flavor Profile:

Rooibos tea is very similar in color and taste to hibiscus tea, however it also has some more earthy flavors, such as the ones you would taste in a yerba mate tea. Similar to its plant structure, rooibos also tastes very woody and nutty, similar to some seasonal "christmas teas."

Medicinal Properties:

One main benefit of rooibos tea is its lack of caffeine and tannins. This makes it a perfect transition drink for coffee, or a drink for later at night. Many people also use this plant for weight and diabetes management. Rooibos has been shown to lower bad cholesterol and raise good cholesterol, in addition to managing and maintaining a healthy heart and circulatory system.

Tea Plant

Description:

The tea plant produces alternating, elliptical leaves. The tea plant's leaves are green in color and have sharp, serrated edges. It grows as a small shrub, and is native to some regions in Asia. The tea plant also grows white flowers that have a strong fragrance.

Cultivation and Parts Used:

Tea plants prefer a sandy, well drained soil. They also thrive in more acidic soil environments. Many people use sphagnum moss when potting their tea plants. It is also recommended to wait a long period (1-3 years) before harvesting your tea plant for internal use. While the majority of the plant is edible (leaves, flowers, etc.), it is customary to consume the leaves in a variety of ways. Many people like to eat the tea leaves on their own in a solid state, as they can yield more nutrients this way. In any case, for a tea you can use the fresh leaves or dry the tea leaves (and even try roasting them for different tea varieties).

Flavor Profile:

Green tea leaves tend to taste earthy, yet sweet. Depending on how they are prepared (powdered and mixed, steeped whole, etc.), the flavor of the tea can drastically change.

Medicinal Properties:

The green tea plant is regarded as one of the most potent antioxidant herbs. Many people utilize this plant (in solid and liquid form) to boost immunity and prepare for upcoming cold seasons. The green tea plant also contains caffeine. This makes it a common switch from coffee, which can be irritating to some individuals. It is also believed that the tea plant boosts catechins (phenols) that can speed up metabolism (and be diuretic), enhancing weight loss.

Dandelion

Description:

Dandelion is a perennial that grows on a thick tap root. It has deeply cut leaves that grow from the ground (not from the main stem). In addition   to this, they are characterized by many bright yellow pedals, and white, airborne seeds. They also produce a white latex that can seep out when the plant is cut.

Cultivation and Parts Used:

In North America, most people consider dandelions to be invasive weeds. Because of this, they can grow pretty rampant anywhere, so you can even find them naturally growing in your neighborhood or your backyard. The whole of the dandelion plant can be used in many ways. Like most plants you can use them fresh or dry, however fresh is best if they are naturally growing near you.

Flavor Profile:

Dandelions have a very bitter and earthy taste. They are very similar in ways to vegetables such as radishes. Dandelions are notably more bitter the longer they grow. People tend to combat this by harvesting them earlier in the season and eating them in salads and other dishes. The dandelions root is the main part used in tea, however it is one of the most bitter portions of the plant.

Medicinal Properties:

Dandelion (mainly the root) is known to be a very strong diuretic in the body, being able to manage many symptoms such as high blood pressure, heart failure and liver disease. Dandelion also contains many essential minerals and nutrients. Lastly, there also has been promising research surrounding the dandelion plant and its ability to prevent/combat cancer cells.

Lavender

Description:

Lavender is a bushy shrub plant that grows in long stems topped with fragrant flowers. These flowers are in purple sprigs at the top of the long stems. After a few years of growing and pruning, many lavender plants begin to grow woody. The lavender plant also lives for a very long time, having an average harvesting lifespan of 20-30 years.

Cultivation and Parts Used:

Lavender prefers a well drained soil and full sun. However, if you are planting a very hot, very sunny environment, somewhere with afternoon shade would probably be the best location to plant. Lavender tends to like neutral soils so don't over-fertilize before or after planting. The stems, flowers and leaves are all edible in the lavender plant. You can use them fresh (as buds or full flowers) or dried for many foods and beverages.

Flavor Profile:

Lavender has a very floral, perfume like scent and taste. On the other hand, the taste of lavender does have hints of mint and rosemary as well, making it a very balanced and palatable flavor. Lavender's unique sweet flavor is commonly used with other summer herbs to make fruity drinks such as lemonade and tea.

Medicinal Properties:

Lavender is thought to be anti-inflammatory and antiseptic, making it a common scent/herb to put on minor cuts and bug bites to speed the healing process. Research also suggests that lavender is very calming and soothing, and might even be helpful for people with mild depression. For this reason, people use lavender as a frontrunner herb in many of their night time tea blends.

Calendula

Description:

Calendula is a very aromatic herbaceous perennial. The calendula plant is very short lived in it's season. Its leaves are commonly found on opposite sides of the stems. The rounded flowers grow out of a central disc and are often used as garnishes in salads or fruity desserts.

Cultivation and Parts Used:

Calendula plants like full sun or part-shaded areas. They however will not tolerate very hot summer heat, and they prefer a late spring, early fall type of environment. When first planted, they should be kept moist, and after becoming acclimated, they should only be watered when the soil becomes dry again. Stress (overwatering, overheating, etc.) will cause the flower heads to droop and go to seed. Harvesting is just like picking/cutting any flower off of its stem, don't be afraid to overcut, as pruning these plants tends to only make them grow more.

Flavor Profile:

Calendula tea is often described as sweet and spicy like their fragrance, with hints of bitterness. Many people pair honey with this tea to complement it's earthy and flowery flavors.

Medicinal Properties:

Calendula is antifungal, antibacterial, and anti-inflammatory. Many people use it/it's oil to heal small flesh wounds, or to soothe overactive eczema. Overall, the main benefits of calendula (as an oil) are for the skin. Many people also drink it in tea for the taste and the calming effects.

Part 3: Tea Additives

Tea Additives:

Tea additives are combined with your store bought or home blended tea to cause a variety of effects. These effects can range from boosting health benefits of the tea, to making it simply taste better. Either way, for the most part these additives are meant to complement or improve the tea, rather than "covering" or "blocking" anything in it. Some examples of these tea additives are honey, sugar and even bee pollen. In this part of the book, we will talk about these additives, how they affect the tea, and their possible medicinal benefits.

Implementing the Additives:

For the most part, the additives are fairly easy to use and add to your teas. Some basic ways of adding these ingredients is through steeping, mixing, and straining. For steeping, you can add the ingredients (such as honey or other plant material) during the steeping time to include it into the tea. This is the easiest to do because it combines the process of steeping the tea, and adding sweeteners or other ingredients. Next is mixing, where you take the additive and mix it in the tea after steeping. Typically you do this with a granulated additive such as sugar, until it is fully dissolved into the tea. Lastly you have straining, this can be used for solid additives (such as other plant material or possibly bee pollen). You strain it into the tea by placing it into a separate tea bag or strainer (mix it with some water if desired) and squeeze the additives so its oils/liquid goes into the tea. Some additives are a little harder to mix into tea. For example stevia powder (straight from the leaf) normally will not mix into liquids such as tea. For additives such as this, you have to make a simple syrup with the stevia (or regular sugar if desired) and water.

Sourcing the Additives:

For most tea additives such as honey or sugar, they are very easy to source from the store or local sellers near you. For other additives, it might be easier or cheaper to grow them yourself. The main example of this is stevia, which can be quite rewarding to grow. Either way, the process in which you acquire your additives is fully up to your personal values/needs. However, most agree that it is always best to buy local/organic or grow them yourself for environmental reasons.

Tea Additives: Specific Ingredients

Honey:

Honey is a very common additive for tea. Honey is antifungal and antibacterial. People usually melt honey into their tea while the water is hot, making it fully mix with the tea. Many people add honey to their tea either to sweeten it naturally, or to help soothe a sore throat during colds and other illnesses

Sugar:

Sugar is very common to add to tea. Specifically, many people add sugar to their tea when it is a very bitter or dark tea. Ice tea is probably one of the most popular teas made with sugar (and normally lots of it). While sugar can make your teas very palatable, it has virtually no health benefits and can be very unhealthy in high doses. For these reasons, it is always best to try to cut down on sugar, or find different natural sweeteners for your teas.

Bee Pollen:

Bee pollen has become a very popular health food, and additive to tea. There are multiple ways to incorporate this ingredient into your tea, such as steeping it, straining it or mixing it in. Bee pollen is shown to have many vitamins, minerals, and antioxidants. It is best to add this to colder teas or to add it later on, as some people believe that the bee pollen tends to become less potent when heated to high temperatures.

Citrus:

Citrus is a great additive to include in your teas. There are many fruits in the citrus family that are great to add to teas, such as lemons, limes, and oranges. Citrus tends to make your tea a little more sweet (naturally) while also adding some sourness to your tea. The citrus fruits also make your tea more acidic, which can allow more catechin molecules to be taken into your small intestine. They also are great sources of fiber in your tea. You can place a slice of a citrus fruit in your tea after/during brewing, place citrus rinds into your steeping bag, or even squeeze a little citrus in your finished tea. To sum it up, citrus is a very healthy/lively tea additive.

Berries and Fruits:

Many teas are very bitter, or have a very distinct flavor profile that requires something sweet. Berries and other fruits are the perfect tea additive for these drinks. Some great examples of these additives are blackberries, raspberries, and apples. These fruits are not only very healthy and full of antioxidants, but they also make your tea very sweet and delicious.

Cinnamon:

Cinnamon is very anti-inflammatory and antioxidant. Many people associate and use this spice in holiday and seasonal teas. Specifically people associate this spice heavily with Fall and Christmas drinks. Cinnamon powder is great to stir into tea as an additive, however it does need a good amount of stirring before it will fully dissolve into the water. Cinnamon pairs well with chocolate, pumpkin, vanilla, chai, and orange blends.

Ginger:

Ginger is another great spicy tea additive. It works similar to cinnamon in many tea blends. Ginger can be added in the steeping, or as a paste/liquid after steeping. Ginger has a very spicy and earthy flavor that works well with other spicy tea blends. Ginger is shown to help with illnesses, especially those that give you nausea. It also can help clear sinuses when you are congested, similar to mint or other similar herbs.

Maple Syrup:

Maple syrup may sound unfitting in tea, however it is very similar to simply adding sugar. Maple syrup of course has more warm, fall flavors than sugar does. Maple syrup, while not healthy, may have more benefits when compared to regular sugar. While normally it doesn't have too many antioxidants or other specific health benefits, when bought locally or organically, it can have a lot of nutrients like zinc and magnesium.

Milk:

Any type of milk can be added to your teas. Many people drink morning teas such as earl gray with splashes of milk. The milk often is added straight to the tea (not heated like with coffee). The milk added to tea is very similar to coffee, giving it a creamier, fuller taste in the end.

Part 4: Basic Tea Recipes

Basic Tea Recipes:

In this section, we will talk about a few basic tea recipes that you can use every day. These recipes will be broken down by what ingredients you use, what flavors you want to taste, and even what health benefits it may offer to you. Lastly, these recipes will be mostly in random order, but mostly similar teas will be grouped together in this list.

Disclaimer:

As a warning, while these teas are meant to be for enjoyment and health, some flavors/reactions may not agree with you. It is always good to start slow with your teas, with small amounts of tea and small amounts of ingredients. This is so you will be introduced to the flavors and how they affect you in a small amount. With these recipes, if you are allergic to an ingredient, or simply don't like it, feel free to substitute in or even remove it!

Customizing generalities:

As stated earlier, with these tea recipes, you can fully build off of them, replacing or adding ingredients to your pleasure. There are a few generalities that you should follow while customizing teas, so that you will enjoy every cup of tea. First of all, you should mainly try to only include 1-2 harsh flavors in your teas when you are just starting out, this ensures that you can actually still drink your cup of tea when it turns out. Next, you should try to keep within the flavor profiles you have the recipe in, unless you specifically like differing flavors. This generality is in place because not many people like to have summery berry flavors mixed in with spicy winter flavors. Lastly and most importantly, while teas can be very healthy and even fight illness, it is always important to keep taste in mind throughout the whole process. There is nothing worse than making a tea to benefit your health and then having it taste like spicy mud. Overall, the main takeaway message here is to always remember that even if you are using medicinal ingredients, the end result should always strive to be tasty and enjoyable.

Fall Spiced Apple Tea:

This tea is a great callback to warm fall apple cider. Perfect for watching a fall storm, or simply enjoying while sitting up next to a fireplace. It brings the sweetness of apple juice to the spicy warmth of cinnamon and other spices.

Ingredients:

- Apple Juice
- Cloves
- Cinnamon
- Apple slices/Cinnamon sticks (optional)

Brewing Instructions:

Bring water to a boil in a large saucepan or pot. Add in your cloves and cinnamon (and any other additives or spices). Bring the water to a boil and stir occasionally to ensure that the tea steeps and is properly mixed. When the tea is brewed to a semi-strong level, take off the heat and stir for 30 seconds to 1 minute. While the tea is warm, pour in apple juice to taste. Note that while you want the tea to have a sweet apple taste, less is best with the proportions of juice. After thoroughly mixing, you can choose to add extra ingredients to the tea, such as a slice of apple in the glass, cinnamon sugar on top, or even a stick of cinnamon.

Medicinal/Health Properties:

As shown before, cinnamon is a very beneficial spice, with lots of health properties. Similarly, clove also has many health properties, most notably being a strong antibacterial. Other than using this tea to help enjoy the fall and winter season, it is a great tea to drink when you feel a little low. Not only does the apple juice provide sugar and fruit nutrients, but the spices also help to fight off bacteria and other illnesses when you are sick. In addition to this, the spices in this tea are also very anti-inflammatory, making them very common in weight loss teas.

Spiced Citrus Honey Tea:

This tea is a great one to include in your fall/winter recipes when you want something other than cinnamon. While it still has some spice in it, the flavor profile more heavily sways to the citrus fruits.

Ingredients:

- Honey
- 1 Orange
- 1 Lemon
- Cloves
- Cinnamon

Brewing Instructions:

Begin by skinning the orange and lemon. Bring water to a high temperature (175+) and place the citrus rinds, cloves and cinnamon into the water. Keep on heat for five or more minutes while stirring off and on. When at desired concentration, take off heat and stir for another minute. Pour or strain into a cup or mug of your choosing. After this you can squeeze your lemon and orange into the cup, or place them in or on the rim of the cup. Then pour some honey into the tea and stir until fully dissolved.

Medicinal/Health Properties:

Similar to other winter teas, this recipe holds similar properties to the other spiced teas. It's anti-inflammatory and great for when you are feeling down and have a cold. As for the citrus, they are great in this tea because they are low calories and provide a lot of beneficial nutrients. They provide fibers, vitamins and much more. Overall, this tea, like other winter teas, is great for when you have a cold, or just for when you want to get into the Christmas or Halloween spirit.

Turmeric Golden Milk Tea:

Similar to western chai tea, golden milk tea has become very popular nowadays. It originated from India and is highly revered now for its medicinal properties and taste.

Ingredients:

- Milk or Milk Substitute
- Cinnamon or a Cinnamon Stick
- Turmeric
- Ginger
- Honey
- Black Peppercorns
- Cloves
- Coconut Oil (Optional)

Brewing Instructions:

Pour milk into your saucepan or pot. Note: in this recipe, the milk stands in place of the water, so however much milk you use, is however much tea you get. Place all of your ingredients into the pan. For ingredients such as ginger and cinnamon, you can choose which form you use (for example: cinnamon sticks and cinnamon powder). Bring this mixture to a low boil (as not to burn the milk) and continuously stir. When the color starts to change and the milk starts to boil, lower the temperature to a simmer. Continue mixing on simmer until you get the desired concentration. Strain into your cup or mug (note you will have to strain well/multiple times as most of the ingredients are hard to get out). After the tea is in a cup, you can add toppings such as whipped cream or cinnamon sugar.

Medicinal/Health Properties:

Most of the spices in this tea recipe are anti-inflammatory and full of antioxidants. This tea is a great health booster as it is full of natural immune boosters. This recipe also holds unique benefits with the use of coconut oil. For example, using coconut oil (such as swishing with the oil itself) can kill harmful bacteria in the mouth, improve gum health, soothe swelling gums, reduce bad breath, and even whiten teeth in the long run. In the end, this tea mixes the benefits of cinnamon tea blend, with the benefits of coconut oil and natural fats.

Chocolate Mint Tea:

Chocolate mint tea provides the health benefits of natural herbs such as mint, while including the luxurious tastes of cacao and spice. It is a very simple tea with few ingredients, however mixing with flavors such as lemon and orange, the possibilities with this recipe are endless. While this tea blend can use any variety of mint, chocolate mint or spearmint is the best option as it mixes best with the natural flavor of cacao.

Ingredients:

- Mint (of any variety)
- Cinnamon
- Cacao nibs
- Chocolate (optional)

Brewing Instructions:

Place water and ingredients in a pot and bring to a high temperature, but not a boil. Mint leaves can burn easily and give a more bitter taste to the tea, which is not desired in this case where we are trying to achieve a sweeter, chocolate taste. Stir every once in a while until the desired concentration is reached. Strain and pour into a cup.

Medicinal/Health Properties:

This tea is a great way to get the many health benefits of mint, while being able to enjoy a more chocolate heavy drink. The mint in this tea is great for the digestive system. It can help sooth a sore stomach and settle your nerves. While there isn't a lot of caffeine in cacao nibs, this tea still isn't necessarily recommended for a nighttime blend. This is simply because there are other tea blends such as plain mint and chamomile which work much better in nighttime tea blends.

Matcha Mint Iced Tea:

The matcha mint iced tea is a great recipe if you want to get the benefits of mint and matcha, while having the cool refreshing feeling of summer drinks. This tea is also great for people who don't like warm matcha or tea, but still want to have the full flavor without ice dilution.

Ingredients:

- Matcha powder (around 1 tsp per cup of water)
- Ice

- 1 Lime
- 1 Lemon
- Mint

Brewing Instructions:

Place matcha powder into water in a shakable container or a large cup. Shake until the tea turns bright green in color. If you are using a cup instead of a container, whisk thoroughly until this green color is met. Strain or pour into a cup or mug and squeeze or place the sliced lemon and lime in with the matcha. Muddle the mint (or squeeze before mixing) and place in the glass as well. Lastly, use ice to cool off your drink to your temperature preferences.

Medicinal/Health Properties:

Matcha is definitely one of the most beneficial health teas. It is thought to fight heart disease, cancer, diabetes, and even aid in weight loss. These health benefits are thought to come from the catechins in the tea. In addition, matcha has more caffeine than green tea, but less than coffee, making it a perfect medium for people who find coffee to be too stimulating. In addition, the mint has calming properties to the nervous and digestive systems. Overall, this tea is best for early morning to mid-day, as the caffeine may affect some people more than others. It is a great drink to have with bigger meals or in the summer as it can calm the digestive system.

Calming Mint Tea Blend:

Similar to the other mint tea blends, this tea is a great nighttime beverage. Mint is very versatile as when paired with citrus and fruit, it has a summer quality, and while paired with chocolate and spice, it has a winter quality.

Ingredients:

- Mint (of any variety)
- Lemon Balm
- 1 Lemon
- Lavender
- Valerian Root (optional)

Brewing Instructions:

Remove the rind from the lemon and place it in a pot or saucepan of water with the rest of the ingredients. Brew on a medium high temperature (180 or below) so as to not burn the lighter ingredients such as lavender. When the tea reaches the desired concentration, strain into a cup. Place a slice of the lemon or squeeze some juice into the tea and enjoy!

Medicinal/Health Properties:

This tea provides many benefits along with its calming effects. Most of the ingredients work to soothe the nervous system and calm the mind. Together they work very well to help aid insomnia. In addition the mint is a great stomach settler, making it a perfect cup of tea to have late at night, after dinner, before bedtime. The strongest ingredient in this tea is the valerian root, which contains hesperidin and linarin. These antioxidants are shown to slow amygdala activity, which is the center for fear and stress responses. Due to this ingredient, the tea is also great as a minor anti-anxiety supplement.

Love Is In The Air Blend:

This tea utilizes the natural flavors in flowers to soothe the nervous system. Not only does this tea help the mind, but it also is very healthy for the heart.

Ingredients:

- Rose petals

- Rose hips (optional)
- Lavender
- 1 Lemon
- Lemon Balm

Brewing Instructions:

Place all ingredients except the lemon into a pot of water. If you are using fresh rose petals (from the stem), remove the petals and use them alone. Use medium heated water (130-160 degrees) as these lighter ingredients can burn and turn bitter easily. Strain into a glass and squeeze the lemon juice into the tea.

Medicinal properties:

Similar to other mint teas, this blend is a great nighttime beverage. All of the ingredients are well known herbs and plants that help calm the nerves and help people fall asleep. In addition to this, the rose petals (and rose hips) are also great plants for the heart. They also lower cholesterol, helping heart health that way as well. Lastly, they are simply well known to have minor antidepressant qualities, lifting the spirits in times of need.

Respiratory Health Tea:

The respiratory health tea blend is perfect for maintaining healthy lungs during a strong cold season. In addition, it also is fairly good at helping the body fight off colds or other illnesses that affect the lungs specifically. In this recipe, there will be many common herbs, meaning there are many possible variations of the plants available.

Ingredients:

- Thyme
- Rosemary
- Mint
- Sage

Brewing Instructions:

Place all ingredients in water and bring to a high temperature (180+). Strain when the desired concentration is met and enjoy!

Medicinal/Health Properties:

All of the ingredients in this tea are well known for being beneficial to the respiratory system. Many of the herbs, such as thyme are also great at expelling mucus, making them great herbs to include in a cold fighting blend. Overall, these herbs in a tea can be used to maintain respiratory health in allergy/cold seasons, or help the body fight off an existing respiratory illness.

Feminine Health Blend:

This blend is used to help balance the body during a woman's natural cycle. Of course while effects may vary, this tea can balance hormones to reduce period pain and mood swings. It can also help encourage nervous system balance, and lessen the discomfort of menopause.

Ingredients:

- Valerian Root
- Dandelion root
- Burdock Root
- Rose Petals
- Ginger
- Orange Peel
- Cinnamon
- Blackberry Leaf
- Raspberry Leaf

Brewing Instructions:

Combine ingredients to your taste and bring to a low boil. Keep on heat until concentration meets your taste (although longer is best with this blend). Bring off of heat and strain into a mug. Top with cinnamon (or cinnamon sugar) for a sweeter taste.

Medicinal/Health Properties:

The feminine health blend is a perfect tea to help with monthly cycles or menopause. Some specific properties are the tannins and vitamins. For example, the blackberry leaf has many tannins and vitamin C, thought to help with period pain, along with other symptoms such as a sore throat. In addition, the raspberry leaf not only helps with menstruation as well, but it also has been used to ease pains during labor and delivery. Lastly, some ingredients such as valerian root have been included for their mild sedative and pain reducing properties.

Vitamin C Tea:

This tea is meant to boost and maintain vitamin C levels. Vitamin C is known to protect cells, and improve skin, blood vessels, cartilage, and bone,

Ingredients:

- Rose Petals
- Hibiscus
- Dried Berries (Raspberry, Blackberry, Etc.)
- Orange Peels
- Lemongrass
- Coriander
- White Tea (optional)

Medicinal/Health Properties:

As previously stated, this tea is simply meant to maintain and boost vitamin C levels. Out of the ingredients, rose petals and coriander are shown to have the most vitamin C (however most of the ingredients contain notable amounts of it). In addition, some ingredients such as orange peels and lemongrass are also added for their sweet citrus taste, which is the main theme of the blend. Overall, with the vitamin C in this blend, the medicinal goal is to improve skin, as well as internal workings such as the circulatory system.

Energize Tea Blend:

This blend is meant to wake you up on those tough mornings to help you feel energized. It has a sweet, citrus and rose taste, making it very enjoyable.

Ingredients:

- Ginger
- 1 Orange
- 1 Lemon
- Rose Petals
- Lemongrass

- Cinnamon
- Rosemary
- Thyme

Brewing Instructions:

Begin by peeling some skin off of your lemon and orange (if you don't wish to brew whole slices). Place all of the ingredients into a pot of water and bring to a high temperature (180+ degrees). When the tea reaches the desired concentration, take off of heat and stir for 1-2 minutes. Strain into a cup or mug and enjoy.

Medicinal/Health Properties:

Similar to a vitamin C tea blend, this tea has rose, orange, and lemon which all contain lots of vitamin C (and D). The citrus fruit is also very warming to the body, being able to energize you without any caffeine.

Runner's Tea:

This tea is designed to help aid in recovery after long runs of physical activity.

Ingredients:

- Dandelion Root
- Peppermint
- Skullcap
- Nettle Leaf
- Valerian Root
- Licorice Root
- Lemon Balm

Brewing Instructions:

Squeeze the lemon balm and peppermint before brewing. Place all ingredients in a pot with water and bring to a medium high temperature (160-180 degrees). Steep for at least 3 minutes stirring every 30 seconds (if steeping in a pot). Strain into a cup and enjoy.

Medicinal/Health Properties:

This tea is great for recovering from extraneous physical activity. It is also great for athletes who do prolonged physical exercise such as runners and swimmers. The tea provides specific nutrients that help support the muscular, nervous, and skeletal system, especially during recovery. In addition, ingredients such as valerian root and peppermint are included to dull any aches or pains and to help cool down and get rest after physical activity.

Kidney/Bladder Health Tea:

This tea is meant to promote and maintain kidney and bladder health. It also is specifically meant to prevent unwanted bacteria from travelling into the urinary tract. The flavor is grassy and semi-sweet. If a sweeter taste is desired, try adding honeybush or rooibos (along with a sweet tea additive).

Ingredients:

- Dried Cranberries
- Dried Blackberries
- Dried Raspberries
- Nettle Leaf
- Dandelion Leaf
- Honeybush (optional)
- Rooibos (optional)

Brewing Instructions:

Place all ingredients into a pot of water and brew at a medium-high temperature (160-180 degrees). Stir thoroughly while and after brewing. When the desired concentration is reached, strain into a cup.

Medicinal/Health Properties:

In this tea, the cranberries hold the main properties that help prevent infection. They contain proanthocyanidins that prevent bacteria from entering and attaching to the lining of the urethra and bladder. Additionally, nettle leaf in this blend is used as a diuretic to flush the kidneys and treat kidney stones.

Citrus Twist Blend:

This tea is mainly meant for pure enjoyment, however many of the ingredients also contain specific vitamins and nutrients that can aid the body in everyday functions.

Ingredients:
- 1 Lemon
- 1 Lime
- 1 Orange
- Lemon Balm
- Mint (citrus variety preferred)
- Dried Berries (Raspberries, Blackberries, Etc.)

Brewing Instructions:

Peel your citrus fruits (if you don't want to steep whole slices) and set aside everything but the rinds. Place the rinds (or slices) and all other ingredients in a pot and heat water to a high temperature (180+ degrees). Stir occasionally to ensure the vital oils infuse out of the rinds. When a dark orange/green is met, take off of heat and strain into a cup.

Medicinal/Health Properties:

The citrus in this tea provides many nutrients, vitamins and fiber, making it a great overall health tea. They can also boost heart health and aid in kidney functioning. While this tea has lemon balm and mint added, it is not necessarily a night time tea, as the bright citrus flavors are stimulating and balance out the calming effects.

Standard Chai:

This is a standard recipe for a chai tea. Using this base, you can create a plethora of different teas based on your taste preferences and available local herbs. In addition, this recipe uses a chai base that is mixed with other ingredients to actually make the chai tea.

Ingredients:
- Ginger
- Fennel Seeds
- Cardamom
- Cinnamon
- Cloves
- Black Pepper
- Honey

- Milk
- Bay leaves (optional)
- Black Tea (optional)

Brewing Instructions:

Begin by making the chai base. To do this, combine all the spices into a mix (not including the milk, honey, or black tea). Combine 2 teaspoon of spice mix to every cup of water in concentrate. Bring to a low boil and simmer for 20+ minutes (or less depending on preference). Do this in a covered pan to prevent evaporation. After preparation, store it in a container for use. To make the chai, combine chai base and milk in a saucepan, and bring the mixture to a medium heat. After heating, add honey and black tea and let steep for 4+ minutes. Strain into a cup and enjoy!

Medicinal/Health Properties:

Due to the spices in this tea such as cinnamon, this tea is great for digestion and can even help aid with weight loss. Other than this, it is a great tea to help lift the spirits during the cold fall and winter months.

Sore Throat Kicker:

This infusion mix is blended to help with sickness. Specifically, sicknesses that cause sore throats and respiratory symptoms.

Ingredients:

- Rose Petals
- Cinnamon
- Lemon Peel
- Licorice Root
- Ginger
- Marshmallow Root (optional)
- Orange Peel (Optional)

Brewing Instructions:

Separate the petals from the rosebuds and the rind from the lemon if you are using whole natural ingredients. Brew all of the ingredients in a pot with water on medium-high heat. When the desired concentration is met, remove from heat and strain into a cup.

Medicinal/Health Properties:

In this recipe, the volatile oils from the lemon (and orange) work to help coat
the throat to relieve pain. In addition, other ingredients such as ginger and
cinnamon work to soothe inflamed tissue, caused by other cold/illness
symptoms. Rose petals are also antiseptic, making them great for coating and
preventing further problems to the throat.

Cold Kicker Tea:

Similar to the sore throat kicker tea, this tea is meant to help the body during
sickness. Rather than focusing on coating the throat, this blend is meant to
fuel the body to help it recover, while relieving some common cold
symptoms. In this blend, the optional ingredients are those that relieve pain
and can help you fall to sleep, similar to over the counter cold medications.

Ingredients:

- Mint (Peppermint preferred)
- Echinacea
- Ginger
- 1 Lemon
- Lemon Balm
- Cherry tree Bark (optional)
- Valerian Root (optional)

Brewing Instructions:

Begin by peeling the lemon if brewing whole slices isn't desired. Then place
all ingredients into a pot of water (or tea bags respectively). If you wish to get
the most out of ingredients such as mint or lemon balm (fresh), try agitating
them to let some of the oils and scents out. Then brew on a medium-high heat
for at least 5 minutes. When desired concentration is reached, strain in a mug
and enjoy!

Medicinal/Health Properties:

Many of the ingredients in this tea, such as echinacea are well known for
being immunostimulants. This can help spur on the immune system during a
cold, or even keep it healthy and ready to fight one during cold seasons.
Other herbs such as lemon balm and mint are supposed to lift the spirits and

decongest the nasal passages. Lastly, the optional ingredients are known to help ease pain and help people fall asleep (especially when recovering from a cold).

Cancer Care Blend:

This tea blend is meant to support anyone recovering or currently going through cancer treatment. It's ingredients offer help with the immune system, and help with adapting to further stress on the body.

Ingredients:

- Fennel
- Linden
- Licorice Root
- Tulsi
- Lemon Balm
- Mint
- Chamomile
- Ginger
- Cinnamon (optional)

Brewing instructions:

Place all ingredients in a pot with water. For ingredients like mint and lemon balm, try agitating them before use to release the volatile oils. Brew on a medium-high heat for 5 or more minutes. Strain into a cup and enjoy!

Medicinal/Health Properties:

The ingredients in this tea are meant to provide full body support and care during cancer recovery and treatment. Herbs such as chamomile and lemon balm are nervous system calmers that help reduce stress responses in the body. In addition, adaptogen herbs such as licorice root and tulsi help the body respond to stress and adapt to new stressful situations such as cancer treatment. Lastly, ingredients such as cinnamon and ginger help prevent further infections/illnesses due to having strong anti-inflammatory properties.

Pregnancy Tea:

This tea is meant to support the body during pregnancy. Pregnancy teas contain rich vitamins, minerals and nutrients that are meant to support the body while carrying a child. While these teas are mainly made with well known, safe herbs, it is always good to check allergies and consult your doctor, especially during such a vulnerable process.

Ingredients:

- Raspberry Leaf
- Blackberry Leaf
- Peppermint
- Rose petals
- Chamomile
- Dandelion Leaf
- Nettle Leaf

Brewing Instructions:

Place all ingredients in a pot full of water (or tea bags if that is the preferred brewing method). For aromatic herbs such as mint, try agitating them before brewing to release more volatile oils. Brew on a low to medium heat for at least 3 minutes. When desired concentration is met, strain and drink.

Medicinal/Health Properties:

Blackberry and raspberry leaves are full of vitamin B, C, and E, along with many other nutrients. Due to this, they are thought to help reduce labor time, help labor pains, and facilitate postpartum recovery. Along with having many vitamins and nutrients, dandelion leaf is shown to help relieve water retention, as one would experience during pregnancy. Overall, this tea blend contains many vitamins, minerals and nutrients which are thought to relieve many different symptoms of pregnancy.

Summer Tea Blend:

Focusing less on the medicinal side, this tea is supposed to harness the natural flavors of summer to create a refreshing (often iced) drink.

Ingredients:

- 1 Lemon
- 1 Lime
- Lemon Balm

-   Mint (of any variety)
-   Berries (Raspberries, Blackberries, Cranberries, etc.)
-   Rose petals (optional)
-   Fruit Juice (optional)

Brewing Instructions:

Peel the lemon and the lime, if brewing whole slices isn't preferred. Place all ingredients (other than fruit juice) into a pot of water to brew. For the lemon balm and mint, try agitating them before brewing to help release more volatile oils and flavor. Brew at a low to medium temperature for at least 5 minutes. Try brewing to a more concentrated level, if fruit juice is going to be used in the recipe. When desired concentration is met, strain into a cup and mix with fruit juice until preferred sweetness is achieved.

Medicinal/Health Properties:

While this tea focuses less on medicinal value, it still holds many nutrients and health benefits. For example, the citrus fruits help provide additional fiber and vitamins to one's diet. Also using specific berries such as cranberries can help support urinary tract health. Other than being very refreshing in the summer months, ingredients such as mint and lemon balm can also help calm the nerves, or get one ready for bedtime.

Berry Hibiscus Tea:

Similar to other summer tea blends, this tea is mainly meant to be refreshing during the summer months. It utilizes the natural sweetness of berries and fruits to help quench thirst and refresh the body.

Ingredients:

-   Blackberries
-   Raspberries
-   Raspberry Leaf
-   Mint
-   Lemon Balm
-   Hibiscus
-   1 Lemon

Brewing instructions:

Cut the lemon into slices to brew. Place all ingredients (including some lemon slices) into a pot of water, Bring to a medium-high heat and brew for 4+ minutes. Once the desired concentration is reached, strain into a cup and top with a slice of lemon and a sprig of mint.

Medicinal/Health Properties:

Similar to the last summer tea, this is purely meant for enjoyment. It does however offer some specific health benefits, especially to women. Other than the abundance of vitamins, minerals and nutrients, it offers some reproductive health with the raspberry leaf. In addition, it has a calming effect to the nervous system due to the volatile oils found within the mint and lemon balm.

Wildberry Tea:

This wild berry blend uses the natural flavors of summer berries and their leaves to refresh and cool the body. This tea goes great with additional fruit juices or lemonades as well. Similar to other berry teas, this is great for the summer months as it tends to have a cooling and calming effect on the body.

Ingredients:

- Blackberries
- Raspberries
- Wildberries (of any variety)
- Hibiscus
- 1 Lemon
- Raspberry Leaves
- Blackberry Leaves

Brewing Instructions:

Peel or slice the lemon depending on how you want it brewed. Place all ingredients in a pot of water and brew on medium-high heat. Brew until preferred concentration is reached, then strain and enjoy.

Medicinal/Health Properties:

The berries in this tea provide lots of vitamins and nutrients to the body. They are also very antioxidant and overall healthy for the entire body. Ingredients such as raspberry and blackberry leaves also have many minerals and nutrients, but also support the female reproductive system (before, during, and after pregnancy). Overall this tea holds most of its health benefits in its vitamins and nutrients.

Minty Sun Tea:

As a sun tea, this recipe helps harness the power and energy of the sun into a refreshing beverage. This tea's flavor focuses on mint and other fruit, however altering this recipe can result in a variety of different and wonderful flavor profiles.

Ingredients:

- Mint (of any variety)
- Blackberries
- Lemon Slices
- Honey (optional)
- Ice (optional)

Brewing Instructions:

Agitate mint before brewing. Place the mint, blackberries, and lemon slices into the tea. If desired, honey can be added into the brew as well. Place ingredients and luke warm to semi-warm water in a jar (depending on preference). Seal the jar completely and let sit in the sun for at least 2 hours. When the color develops into a golden red and green hue, drink straight from the jar or strain into a different cup. If tea is preferred cold, add ice and honey.

Medicinal/Health Properties:

With the mint and lemon, this tea is a very good digestive aid. This is especially true when it is brewed for long periods of time, allowing all the essential nutrients and oils to diffuse out of the herbs. Additionally, if honey is added to the tea, it acts as a strong antibacterial. When you drink this tea (or other similar blends) it can help coat sore throats or prevent infections.

Simple Lemon Apple Mint Tea:

This blend is used for people who want the benefits of mint, but don't

necessarily like the taste of it alone in teas. This recipe focuses on the flavors
of apple and how well they pair with mint, however editing the fruit that is
used can create a variety of different flavor profiles. Due to the similar
flavors, apple mint tea is preferred in this recipe, however most mint varieties
tend to work well with most fruit flavors.

Ingredients:

- Mint (of any variety)
- Sliced Apples
- Sliced Lemon
- Lemon Balm
- Honey (optional)
- Apple Juice (optional)

Brewing Instructions:

Begin by preparing the sliced fruit. Place all ingredients (other than apple
juice and honey) into a pot and brew at a medium-high temperature. Allow to
brew for at least 5 minutes. Stir every once in a while to ensure the fruit skins
don't burn. When desired flavor is reached, Strain into a cup and add apple
juice and honey to taste.

Medicinal/Health Properties:

This tea is a very good digestive aid with the mint and lemon balm. It also
has a lot of natural fructose sugars with the various fruits and fruit juices.
Adding honey can make the tea antibacterial, and great for individuals with
sore throats. Overall, this tea also has a lot of vitamins and minerals found in
all of the various fruits and herbs.

Pain Kicker Tea:

This blend is structured to help relieve and ease bodily pain. It can be utilized
during illnesses such as colds that cause aches, or during bouts of physical
pain from injuries that cause inflammation.

Ingredients:

- Mint (of any variety)
- Skullcap
- Licorice Root

- Cinnamon
- Ginger
- Rose Petals
- Cloves
- Lavender
- Sliced Lemon
- Valerian Root

Brewing Instructions:

Begin by agitating fragrant ingredients such as mint to allow their oils to infuse easier. Place all ingredients in a pot of water and brew at a medium-high temperature. Brew for at least 5 minutes and stir occasionally. Add honey or other additives to taste, as this tea can be quite bitter. Strain once the desired concentration is met and enjoy it!

Medicinal/Health Properties:

Ingredients in this tea such as mint and rose petals are shown to be semi anti-inflammatory and also calming, which always helps when one is feeling pain. Next, other ingredients such as valerian root, lavender, and cloves are thought to fight pain (in different areas of the body). Lasty, cloves, cinnamon and ginger also possess anti-inflammatory properties which can help relieve swelling or even ease pain in areas such as the head or limbs. Overall this tea aims to ease pain anywhere in the body, by utilizing multiple different medicinal herbs that have varying effects on the body.

PART 5: GROWING AND CULTIVATING YOUR OWN TEAS

Growing and Cultivating Teas:

In this part of the book, we will discuss all the states of cultivating your own tea. This can range from picking seeds, to general growing tips, to how to dry and store herbs. In all of these situations, your personal preferences and materials always dictate what you should choose. For example, if you are living in a 4th story apartment in New York City, try growing a window box full of herbs, rather than an in-ground garden. No matter how fancy some set-ups may seem, you should always work within your comfortable means to make the best tea you can.

Picking Seeds:

It may seem like a simple, mundane task to pick your seeds, however there are many different varieties and sourcing types, which can make the process rather overwhelming. First of all, on a level of pure preference, you should decide if you want a more natural variety of seeds, or a more processed (but possibly easier to grow) variety. In general, this is referring to whether you want to buy natural (or even local seeds), or if you want to buy a bigger GMO brand. In most cases, this decision fully relies on your values or wants, as the seeds always tend to grow the same (except for GMO seeds that are engineered to be more hardy). In addition to these points, there are actually 3 main types of seeds (including the GMO and naturally sourced). Other than the previous two, there are also hybrid seeds, which come from plants that have been "naturally" cross-bred with other plants in order to attain certain characteristics such as color or smell. These types of seeds refer to ones such as chocolate mint (or any other mint variety), purple sage, and mini pumpkins. These seeds tend to grow really well on their first run, however attempting to yield more seeds from them can be a gamble. Attempting to get seeds from a hybrid plant does not guarantee that the seeds will have the same genes. This is especially true when multiple plants of the same family or genus are held together, such as a bed of different mint varieties.

Lastly for deciding on what seeds you should get, you have to look at a price point and a location for purchasing. First, you should look at the price. While good quality expensive seeds may be natural and great for your garden, a cheaper alternative might grow just as successful for you. The point is to work within your means. You don't need golden gardening tools and premiere seeds to make a good cup of tea. Lastly, you should look at the location in which you are buying the seeds. You can begin by looking online at the options that may be there. This is a good option when you are buying seeds in bulk (or large amounts of multiple seeds), as it often is cheaper, with no shipping costs when you purchase enough. Next you can look at buying them from your local store. These seeds are the most likely to be mass manufactured and GMO. These seeds do work well, however some may not want to purchase this option as it supports a large system that could be improperly mass producing a natural product at the expense of smaller seed companies. Last you can look at local seed companies, or even your friends. These local companies could be in your local stores, or at farmers markets. They normally could cost a little bit more, but the benefit is you know exactly where your seeds are coming from. You can also look and see if your friends or acquaintances have any spare seeds that they are willing to sell, or even give away. This is a great method for people who absolutely have nothing to invest in this hobby, and want to see if it is a good fit for them. Overall, there are so many choices to think about when choosing what seeds to purchase, but in the end it all relies on your location, how many and what type you want to buy.

Planning Your Garden:

Similar to choosing seeds, planning your garden seems fairly simple. Also similarly to seeds, it can be fairly daunting, and there are a lot of things to think about before getting started. In general, when planning your garden, you should think of the location, your budget, the plants you want to grow, and how many plants you want to grow.

To start, you should think of the general location you want to start your garden. With this, you should keep a track of how much sunlight the area you are thinking about gets, especially if it is in a windowsill. The location is probably the most important aspect of planning your garden. It relates to your budget, the plants you want to grow, and how many you want to grow.

Next, you should think about your budget, and it's relation to your garden planning. This is the most restricting category, as in many cases your budget dictates all of the other outcomes in your garden. While it may be fun to splurge on a garden, there are perfectly great options that don't break the bank. For example, many people try to start off with fancy hose heads or drip irrigation systems when there are many lower cost options that can do the same job. In addition to this, there are many low cost (or even free) garden plans that you can use. In fact, many of these DIY garden plans (and tools) can even be beneficial for the environment because they can upcycle old tools and materials. Some examples of these are homemade planters from used materials such as milk and egg cartons.

You also should look at which plants you want to grow. I have personally found no issues with cross pollination or bad plant interactions, however some people live by certains rules that dictate what plants should be grown together. According to these rules, some plants shouldn't be planted together because they can physically hinder each other, or because they can help facilitate disease and pests. For an example of a physical hindrance, some people don't plant tomatoes near smaller plants as they can grow tall enough to fully block the sun from the smaller plant. Many people also recommend growing diverse plants together, as they can make it harder for pests to take over your whole garden. In general, while you should keep this in mind, I have found that it is a minor detail in the process of planning your garden.

Lastly when planning your garden, you should think of how many plants you want to grow. Similar to deciding what plants you should grow, this part of the planning process is a rather minor one. Nonetheless, the number of plants you are wanting to grow can play a part in your planning, as it should dictate how much space you want to allocate for growing. Furthermore, if you are growing herbs, you should also take space into account if you are looking to propagate your plants in the future. Overall, thinking about how many plants you want to grow can heavily affect your garden planning because it dictates the space you should allocate for growing.

In the end, you should evaluate all of the aforementioned criteria as you begin to plan your garden. These topics all dictate how you want to plan your garden, from the space used, to how much money you want to spend on it. While all of these are very important, I am a firm believer that you can make a garden with anything you have on hand, even if it is a singular used nursery pot.

Starting Small:

With gardening (among other tasks), I believe that you should always start small, and work your way up into a bigger job. I also think that you should have the majority of your garden plan fully drafted before you think about starting your garden. I always find that if I attempt to skip a step in the planning process, there is always something that I miss or forget, that always derails my projects. My advice with starting a garden (other than drafting and planning), is to start very small, with one or two plants at the beginning. You should also start with easier and more hardy plants such as mint, especially if you are a first time gardener. While gardening may sound like a fun job, it can be a lot of work, so I also recommend to only work on it a maximum of one to two hours a day. This helps you stay interested in the hobby, and makes sure that you won't get burnt out within the first week or so. You should also start small and slow because gardening takes a lot of patience, especially when you are starting from seeds. In the best case, growing plants (mainly vegetable and other long season herbs) can take at least 1-2 months, if not the whole growing season. To sum up, when starting a garden, you should always take it slow and within your comfort zone.

Alternate Forms Of Starting a Garden:

In addition to starting from seeds, you can also begin your garden in other ways, which can be easier if you are trying to cultivate plants for the first time. First off, you can start your garden from pre-grown starters or full plants. This way is normally the most expensive as sellers add the costs of growing times into their pre-started plants. Depending on the location, these pre started plants can cost anywhere from $2-20 on average. Compared to seeds (which normally cost $1-3), this way is very expensive, particularly if you are looking to purchase multiple plants. On the other hand, buying plants like this gives you very high chances for the plant to grow through the season, or even longer if you play your cards right. In addition to starters, you can also begin your carden through cuttings and other forms of propagation. This form of starting your garden is normally the hardest to do, as in most cases you have to know someone who is willing to let you take cuttings from their pre-grown plants. On the contrary, this way is similar to starting with pre-grown plants, as you are growing off of a base, rather than from a seed. This form also has some problems because propagation can get tricky. If you improperly take a cutting, or dont take care of it immediately after, the cutting can die or get diseased very easily. Ultimately, deciding which method you want to start your garden with is purely up to personal choice, however each method presents it's own benefits and challenges that you should take into account.

Creating Cuttings and Harvesting Herbs:

No matter if you are planning on growing for food, or growing for fun, you should know the basics of creating cuttings for propagating and harvesting general herbs. Normally, you want to use a few basic tools when creating a cutting. These can include, but are not limited to:

- Scissors or Shears (preferably designed for cutting herbs)
- Alcohol or another disinfecting agent
- Rooting hormone gel or powder
- Cinnamon or Honey (optional)

More on the tools, many people like to disinfect their scissors before and after each use, as it prevents infection and disease in the plants that you are cutting. In addition, rooting hormone is used to help facilitate the growth of plant roots, which is especially helpful when starting new cuttings. In addition, I have found that in a pinch (or sometimes in addition to rooting hormone), using cinnamon or honey on cuttings can be helpful because they are also antibacterial and can facilitate root growth. To begin a cutting, I tend to cut above a leaf node (or the growth spot of a leaf), leaving about a 1-2 inch stem from the top of the plant. Then you should strip all of the leaves except for the top 2-4, and place the stem firmly in the ground (or water depending on preference). This general set of steps works for most herbs (including mint, lemon verbena, lavender, etc.), and you can add anything to the steps such as using cinnamon or rooting gel. In addition to this method, you can also place the cutting partially into water in order to form roots. Once they have developed, you can then move them into soil. Most people use this method as it ensures root growth (and you can see it), however I prefer the in-dirt method as it is quicker and has yielded me better results. Lastly on the topic of cuttings and propagation, when trying to duplicate succulents and plants such as aloe vera, you can form cuttings by snipping off a 1-2 inch cutting (or tugging off a leaf) and letting it grow a callous. After the callus has formed, you can then place into dirt like a normal herb cutting and allow for roots to grow. As a word of warning for propagating succulents (particularly aloe vera since it is very moist), you should use some sort of rooting powder, or work in a dry area as they are more likely to rot because it takes longer to form a callus.

On top of creating cuttings, any adept gardener should know how to properly harvest herbs. When harvesting herbs, you should mainly only take what you need (or less), unless the plant you are working with likes regular pruning. For example, with plants such as mint, you should regularly harvest (at least for cuttings) as they thrive off of regular pruning and only grow more and more bushy. Like with everything though, you should always start slow, especially if your plants are new because you don't want to stress them out too much. You should always keep in mind that harvesting plants is a form of damaging them, requiring them to take time and energy to heal. After they are harvested they should be taken well care of, as they are trying to fix the old damage and turn it into newer, bushier growth. In addition, you should study up on your specific plants and keep track of how often they want to be pruned too. Like I said, for mint you can hack away and be rewarded with new abundant growth, but when working with weaker plants, you can be left with a dead withered shrub. Some plants on top of wanting to be pruned less, also want to be pruned less often, only needing/wanting it 1-3 times a season.

As for the specific herb harvesting, you should do it similarly to creating a cutting. By this, I mean you should try to cut above a leaf node so that you will help facilitate further growth. Cutting in this way for most plants allows two new stems to grow from the original cutting spot (because the 2 leaves left over each form into a new stem). In addition to the regular cuttings/harvests, at the end of the season, most plants need a larger pruning/harvest in order to grow best. This not only gives you more output from the plant before the season is over, but it helps weather the plants for the upcoming colder seasons. In the end, you should mainly take only what you need, and unless you are weathering your plant, you should definitely take only 25-40% of the plant or less!

Drying Herbs:

As you begin to harvest your herbs, you will probably find that you will have way too much to use before everything you harvested will rot. One solution to this is drying your herbs for later use. This practice is very common as it is the main way plants are stored in commercial and personal settings. You should also try to dry your herbs as soon as possible from harvesting, because they can rot quickly, or decay from light. Even a little exposure to light can break down certain chemicals in your cut herbs, leaving them less flavorful and medicinally potent. There are a few ways to dry your herbs, but for the most part you can dry your herbs naturally, in the oven, or with a dehydrator. Out of these options, I have found the most success with the natural method. This method is best because it requires no electricity, heat, or other artificial source of drying power. To use this method, depending on the plant, you can take all of your harvested stems, bundle and tiw them with string or twine, and hang them to dry, preferably in a cool, dry, and dark place. You want to try to dry in a cool dark place so that the plants flavor and medicinal compounds are denatured and destroyed. For the most part, this method has yielded me the best results, as there is less of a chance of burning and flavor loss. On the downside, this process can take a very long time depending on the herb (1-3) weeks. In addition, there is a higher chance of mold or other bacteria to form (if not done correctly) because this process takes longer and has less heat involved.

Next up, There is oven drying. I would only recommend using this method for hardy herbs or fruits such as oranges because it is easy to burn lighter plants. Overall, one of the main downsides of this method is that it is really easy to burn the plants you are trying to dry, especially if you lose track of time or are using an older oven. This method is basically the same as the dehydrator method, only cheaper, making it the natural starting place for people who don't have a dehydrator, but who also can't or don't want to take the time to naturally dry their herbs. To use this method, you should bring your oven to a low temperature anywhere from 140-200 degrees fahrenheit. You shouldn't try going over this temperature range as it is the limit for most herbs and fruits (including hardy herbs). Another downside I have found in this method is that your herbs can retain some of the flavors that have been left in your oven from other foods. Due to this, I try to refrain from the oven dehydrating method. On the other hand, this method is good for people who are just starting and don't want to buy a dehydrator because it is fast and can dry more water-dense fruits such as oranges and lemons. In the end, while I don't necessarily recommend this method for long-term gardeners (or most people), it works decently in a pinch, or for people who want to see if they like the hobby of gardening and tea making.

Lastly, there is the dehydrator method. This method is the most expensive because most dehydrators cost at least $40-60. And that number is on the low end, there are some dehydrators that can range from $100-300. Because of this, I would mainly recommend this for people who are very interested in the hobby and know they are going to continue. If you are just starting, I would still recommend the natural or oven method. As you have probably guessed based on the ranging prices, there are many types and models of dehydrators. Personally, I use a basic one within the $40-60 dollar range because for me it gets the job done. Keep in mind, I mainly use my dehydrator for watery fruits and herbs such as lemons, which are harder to burn, and I opt to use the natural method for most of my other plants. In general, the main difference in price points relates to how much the machine can dehydrate and once, and how much control the machine gives you over temperature. Most cheaper machines (such as the one I use) have decent amounts of space, with 4-8 trays to dehydrate at once. On the other hand, most cheaper machines also have little to no temperature control, which can become a problem if you are trying to dehydrate more fragile herbs and fruit. As for the more expensive machines, a lot of them look nicer (more aesthetic for your countertop), have lots of trays to dehydrate, and have very intelligent temperature dials. In the end, if you are planning to dehydrate like me, only using the machine for larger fruits and berries, I would highly recommend purchasing a cheaper machine, as you will require much less temperature control. If you are planning on dehydrating most of your herbs and fruits on a dehydrator, I would then recommend splurging on a more expensive machine, as it will yield better results, especially if you are planning on using the machine for a longer period of time. In general, the main perks of using a dehydrator are that you can dry more herbs very fast, and you don't have to take up kitchen or closet space with bundled herbs. Some of the downsides of this method are that there is a small chance of burning herbs (especially on cheaper machines), and it does take up electricity and can be loud depending on the machine. Lastly, some general advice that I would give is to dry more aerial herbs such as mint, roses, and lavender the natural way because they can be easy to burn, even with the more fancy dehydrators.

Separating Herbs (based on variety):

After your herbs have finished drying or dehydrating, you most likely will have to separate the leaves or flowers from the stem. This of course depends on the type of herbs you're using, but it is in general recommended for most herbs. Almost all herbs grow with leaves growing from a central stem. These herbs include, thyme, mint, rosemary, lavender, and many more. To separate these herbs from the stems, you should pace your fingers below all of the leaves and pinch firmly. While continuing to pinch, you should run your finger down the plant over all of the leaves until they come off. After drying, the leaves will most likely fall off easily, however you may need to still apply some pressure as you separate the leaves, to ensure all the leaves come off. For some hardier herbs that have larger leaves (that are more spread out), I would recommend to just pick the leaves individually because it is normally easier than trying to run your finger down the stem. Some herbs that I would recommend to do this with are stevia and pineapple sage. In addition to this, some herbs I would recommend to separate before drying because they tend to dry awkwardly on the stem. These herbs include sage, pineapple sage, and some varieties of mint. Rather than hanging these to dry, I recommend putting them in a paper bag, or laying them spread out on the counter. When separating larger amounts of herbs, I suggest placing a towel, tarp, or bowl under the area you are working to catch any falling leaves. You can also implement a mesh or strainer of some sort to sift the leaves apart from the stems and other aspects of the plant.

Processing And Storing Your Herbs:

After growing, gathering, and drying your herbs, you then have to plan how you will process and store them. After drying, some people like to place their herbs in the oven on a low temp to kill off any residual bacteria (and to prepare them for later storage). This step isn't necessary, and I normally would not recommend it for any lighter herbs as they can burn very easily, which will ruin the taste in the end run. Otherwise, after your herbs are dried, you can choose what form you want to store your herbs in. By this, I mean you can choose if you want to store your herbs in a whole, powdered, syrup, or mixed form. For the most part, herbs are mainly stored dry and whole (or at least dry and in parts). This is the type of storage you see in everyday herbs from the store such as cilantro or dill, which are dry and in nearly whole parts (or slightly chopped). Next is the powdered form, which I prefer for additives or fruits. For example, I like to dehydrate fresh berries such as raspberries and blackberries, and grind them into a powder to add to drink and food. Adding berries to food in this manner gives them a brighter color and natural sweet flavor. Other than dry forms, you can process your herbs into a syrup or liquid form (such as a vinegar infusion). For a syrup, I tend to take home dried and powdered additive herbs like stevia, and I dissolve them in an equal portion of water to make a sweetener. In other liquid forms such as vinegars and infusions, you would take your herbs and allow them to soak in the liquid for a long time and then usually strain into a separate container for later use. This method is most used for cooking and medicinal procedures where you want a unique flavored oil or vinegar. Lastly, there is the pre-mixed form. This is exactly like a loose leaf tea. It is simply when you pre-mix all of the herbs you want in a tea blend and store them together. This method is great for when you have a recipe you know you love, or when you want to save a little space in your cabinet by combining herbs together.

After you fully process your herbs into the form you want to store them, you then want to have them in a proper container/area for long-term storage. The area and container you use are vital for the storage process as they can make or break the facilitation of your tea's flavor. In this book, I will mainly go in depth on the storage of mixed and dry herbs. However, for herbs you store in a syrup or other liquid format, the only advice I would give is to store in an airtight container (possibly in a dark and dry spot) to prevent early spoilage. As for your dry and mixed herbs, you can store them in a variety of ways such as mason jars, herbal containers, tin cans, etc. In general, there are a few best options, but how you store them is fully depending on your aesthetics, space, and planning. Below is a list of some containers you can store teas in, with a description of how they work, facilitate proper storage:

🖳 Mason Jars

- This container is very common among at-home gardeners and is characterized by a glass vessel with a tin or aluminum top band and lid. It is commonly used for making jams and preserves, but has become very popular with zero-waste communities because they tend to be very aesthetically pleasing and can be used for many purposes (including drinking cups!). For the most part, I would always recommend these containers because they are reusable, known to be of good quality, and I have never had any sealing problems with them. In addition they are very aesthetically pleasing because they show the contents inside, making them great for countertop storage if your cabinet space is stretched thin. On the other hand, since these containers are glass, they do let light come through. This can be a problem if you are storing these for a long period of time (especially on the counter top), because sunlight is known to damage many dried herbs. I would combat this issue by storing them in a cabinet or in a darker area of your kitchen. In the end, I think this is one of the best storage methods because it is multifaceted, zero-waste, and aesthetically pleasing, although in the end, the choice is always up to you!

Aluminum/Other Containers

- Aluminum (or other similar) containers are great options for tea storage. They normally come in an average silver/chrome color, or are plated/wrapped with a label or design. Most tea containers have a rubber gasket system for a lid, which makes them fairly airtight. This makes these containers great for long term storage as they will not let any air in. In addition, since they are not transparent (unlike mason jars) they already block out light which can damage your herbs. Being sleek and normally plain, these tend to look nice on your countertop during storage. Similar to other containers I would still recommend to store in a cooler, dark place just to be safe with your storage. Another great upside to this method is that aluminum is easily recyclable, making it fairly eco-friendly.

- ⬚ Tin Tea Canisters
    - ○ Tin canisters have been the basic storage method for many higher end loose leaf teas. They are very similar to aluminum containers, however they tend to be a little weaker, so they are often mixed with other metals to give them a stronger structure. On the other hand, most people agree that tin is the best for long-term herb storage. Also similar to aluminum, tin is infinitely recyclable and more eco-friendly than plastic. Choosing between tin and aluminum is purely based on choice and aesthetics, but I have mostly found that tin has been the absolute best for long term storage.
- ⬚ Cardboard or Other Papers
    - ○ This is the worst possible option, however in a pinch, it can work for short term storage. I would definitely not recommend using this for any long term storage as it is not good at blocking most air, so the tea will go bad fairly quickly. For the most part, people use paper in storage by creating premade tea bags and boxing them up. In the end, if you were to use this method, I would highly suggest to store in the coolest, driest, and darkest place in your house, so that you will have the highest chances for future success.

While choosing which containers you will use, there are a lot of things to think about. I have a few main recommendations for your storage, which might possibly help you in your decision making. I would say that overall, the temperature and brightness of the area you store in has the largest effect on your herbs. In most cases, you can find a great place to store herbs, which can help supplement your situation if you are trying to store in a lower quality container. I would also suggest trying something eco friendly and reusable, or at least recyclable. In my experiences, I have found that using eco-friendly products and containers (especially in my tea making) has looked the best, and yielded the overall best results.

Continuing the Cycle with Home-Grown Seeds:

At the end of each growing season, there is a small window of opportunity when you can collect various seeds from your plants. Depending on the plant, there are many different ways to harvest and prepare seeds for later growing seasons. I highly suggest to at least try harvesting and growing some of your own seeds, as it can be a very rewarding process. In addition, it normally is great for the local ecosystem as it promotes further plant growth, generates biodiversity and ensures that similar plants will grow in the upcoming years. In general, there are roughly three different broad types of seeds that you can harvest. While this is certainly not very scientifically accurate, I classify the three main seeds types as berries, regular seeds, and large pits. Of course there are many different types of seeds, these I have found to be the most common, especially in tea making, so I decided to simplify the categories to make it easier for our purposes.

First off are berries, which produce some of the smallest seeds. In the wild, berries tend to be eaten by mammals (such as us), then when they are passed through the digestive system, the seeds are fully processed and ready to germinate. This normally helps the berries to spread their genes far and wide, because in the wild, the animal that ate the berry tends to have moved far away, causing another berry plant to sprout in the farther location. This enables berry plants to germinate very fast, and to cover large geographical regions. However, since we are not in the wild, people have to use special techniques in order to harvest seeds from their berry plants. It can be tedious, and many times people like to start with a pre-grown plant because of this. To start the process, you need to have a few ripe berries, you can test their ripeness by squeezing them to feel how firm they are. In this case, the semi-soft (decently ripe) berries tend to work the best. Then you want to mash the berries in order to separate the seeds from the pulp. There are many different ways to do this, and the method you prefer depends on the materials you have. First, you can mash them with a fork manually and sift out or pick the seeds. This can be very time consuming because sometimes the seeds like to hide and stick to the pulp. On the other hand, you can mix them in a blender or hand-pulse mixer until the pulp and seeds naturally separate. Then you would skim the top layer of seeds off and sift or hand pick the rest out. After this, some people like to dry their seeds, but I have found it best for me to simply sow my fresh seeds in compost and wait for them to hopefully sprout. Compost works best for these types of seeds because it can mimic the internal workings of the stomach, enabling seeds to germinate. As I previously said, in the end many people like to let nature happen, or to start these berry plants from larger pre-grown ones, as it can be tedious to do all of the work to get the seeds (especially if it doesn't work out in the end). Luckily, if you live in the northwest (or generally the Pacific Coast), blackberries, and sometimes raspberries grow naturally, making it easy to take a cutting or ask a friend for a plant.

Next up, and most common to cultivate are what I call the "regular plant seeds." These come from most of the herbs I grow for teas, and they are some of the easiest to collect. Some common plants that release these types of seeds are mint, basil, amaranth, and sage. In the wild, these plants bloom and flower, allowing local pollinators such as bees to spread their genes and pollinate surrounding environments. After the plant is pollinated (or after the season ends), the flowers tend to "die off" in a way, leaving a dead looking remnant of the plant. This is the key to your seed collecting, so don't throw away or cut off this part of the plant too soon! When this happens, you will want to wait for most of the plant to follow, so that you won't waste or lose too many seeds while collecting. Next, you want to collect the seeds. To do this, you can cut off the plant heads where the seeds pods (or "dead flowers") are. Then you can place them in a paper bag to store and drop their seeds over the next couple of weeks. After a short time, most of the seeds should have dried and dropped to the bottom of the bag, however you can shake the rest of the plant cuttings to release the rest of the stragglers. Another way you can collect the seeds from the plants is to bring a paper bag straight to the seed pods and shake them into it after you know the seeds are fully developed and dried. This way can be more risky because it is easier to lose seeds in the process of waiting for them to dry and gathering them. Either way, when the seeds are fully dry you can then use them in later seasons (or in a greenhouse setting) to grow more copies of your plants! As a word of warning (and a disclaimer), while trying this with hybrid plants can work for some people, it simply won't always yield results. The hybrid nature of the plants tends to either be sterile (not able to produce working seeds), or tend to grow the parent plant, but not the hybrid. For example, if you gather working seeds from an applemint plant, some of the offspring may be regular mint because it still has the original mint genes in its DNA. In any case, it is great to try this method on your plants because it helps maintain biodiversity, and gives you the chance to make amazing duplicates of your current plant species.

Lastly, there are the seeds that I personally categorize as "larger seeds and pits." These seeds are either of a larger category from fruits like lemons, or they are large pits from foods like avocados. In this category, the process of collection and germination tends to differ from plant to plant, so I will lay out a few generalities and then dive specifically into a few of the common plants and seeds in this category. In general, growing from larger seeds and pits tends to take an extremely long time. It can range from 2-4 weeks for even the smallest of growth when you are starting out. This can be explained because the seeds have a larger case to break out of (like in avocados). This can also be explained because most of these plants also take multiple years (or even decades) to grow into a fully mature plant that bears proper fruit. Many of these plants tend to take a few years (after the original growth) in order to bear fruit. Also in most cases, the first few years of fruit from these plants tend to be slightly inferior to the original. In addition, some fruits from the store are genetically modified, so their seeds won't produce anything, so if you are trying to grow from a store bought fruit I would recommend buying it organically. No matter how hard or long the process takes, I would still recommend everyone to try this, because it is a really fun and rewarding experience in the end, especially when your plant starts to bear fruit, or grow woody branches. That covers most of the generalities of growing from larger seeds and pits, but below I will list and go in depth on how you should go about collecting and growing specific plant species.

- Lemons
  - This is probably the most common large seed plant the people try to grow. In general, it is very easy and often yields great results. I also find that in most cases, it grows fairly fast (but still slow when compared to herbs of a lesser life-span). To start the process, you should get a lemon of good quality. You should also try to get a non-hybrid lemon, as it has better chances of yielding great results. To be safe, you can also purchase organic lemons, or obtain them from a friend, so you know they are GMO or sterile. With lemon seeds, you can plant them right away, or save them for later planting. You should however store the seeds in a moist paper towel (in a dark place). This is because lemon seeds like to stay wet, so if they get dry, the chances of proper germination decreases. For this reason, many people opt to plant straight away. For this set of instructions, I will list out how to plant fresh seeds, however if you are working with store bought or stored seeds, you can follow the same basic set of guidelines.

First, you want to fill a pot full of moist soil. The soil shouldn't be soaking, however it should be moist enough to keep the seeds alive. Then you want to cut open your lemon and obtain some seeds. After, you should place the seed under around .5 inches of dirt, then you can spray with water to ensure the soil is moist enough. Next, you should place plastic wrap over the pot and poke holes for some ventilation. This will allow the pot to function as a greenhouse of sorts to help germinate the seed. Then you should place in a sunny spot and keep watch over it, until the sprout forms. Then remove plastic wrap and continue care, sizing up pots to fit it's ever-growing root structure.

- Avocado
  - This plant grows a fruit that has a very large brown pit in the center. This pit is the seed that you plant to create a new avocado plant. Starting the process for this plant tends to take more time, however in the end it tends to grow similar to a lemon tree. To start the process, you want to get an avocado pit and clean it well. Again, like the other seed growing plants, it's preferable for you to get a pit from an organic or local avocado. Then, you want to determine which end is "up" and "down." To do this, you want to locate the slightly pointier end (which is the top), and place it resting on the flatter end (the bottom). To successfully grow your avocado, you need the bottom to be sitting in water. To do this, most people stick 3-4 toothpicks around the pit (part way in/out) pointing down so that they can put the pit on a cup with the bottom half hanging in water. Then of course, you want to place the put into the cup with just enough water to cover a portion of the bottom of the pit. As your avocado grows roots, you may want to adjust the cup you are using, or the amount of water in the cup. In general, you don't want to drown the roots and make them rot, but you want enough water to keep the roots thoroughly moist. In the end, if any of your avocado roots dry, your plant will almost always die. Then you want to keep doing this process until it grows until 10-15 cm tall. At this point, you can either snip the plant down halfway (to encourage bushiness), or you can place it into soil to grow further. As the plant continues to grow into a tree, you may want to size up pots or place it into the

ground depending on where you live. During the growing process you should continue to pinch every few top leaves off to encourage more fullness in the plant.

- Cherries, Peaches, and Other Small-Medium Pitted Plants
  - Growing cherries, peaches, and other similar plants is the most easy process in the large seed/pit category. In order to grow these, you simply want to place into a mix of compost and soil. This is so the seeds will have assistance in the germination process. Then you want to keep the soil moist until you see sprouts. After this, you want to continue growing like any other seedling. When the plant grows large enough, you can start to trim and prune to promote fullness. Similar to the other larger plants, you will probably want to size up pots or place into the ground depending on your location.

PART 6: WILD HARVESTING AND AN ENVIRONMENTAL TAKEAWAY

Wild Harvesting:

Along with growing or sourcing your own herbs and fruits for teas, you can also try to wild harvest tea ingredients. This depends highly on your location. For example, if you are living in the northwest, you can naturally source and harvest blackberries, stinging nettle, valerian root, and dandelions. These are just a few examples, but depending on your location, you can craft a wide variety of tea blends for various illnesses. Along with this, there are some basics of wild harvesting that you should know that relate to biodiversity, maintaining healthy ecosystems, and personal safety.

Disclaimer: Safety Warning

Like with all other things you put into your body, you should be very cautious because you don't know if you will have a bad reaction. In addition to this, you should be extra careful when wild harvesting because it can be a gamble when identifying species, and you don't know if anything has damaged or tarnished the plant you are planning on ingesting.

Plant Identification:

Plant identification is probably the most important aspect of wild harvesting. It is the one tool you have in order to protect yourself from harmful plant species. For example, one common plant used in medicine is yarrow. Yarrow is characterized by white tufts of flowers coming from a long stem. Similarly, the hemlock plant also has very similar white flowers. The only difference is that yarrow will help stop bleeding, while hemlock will kill you with haste. In general, I like to keep my own log of plants that I wild harvest and pick, so that I have a personalized description and basis to go off of in future harvests. In addition, I would recommend using at least 3 or more sources when identifying a plant species, so you will have 100% confidence that the plant you have yields the correct results and doesn't harm you.

10-25% rule:

This is a very basic rule I use when wild harvesting, but it can be the difference between helping and harming a local ecosystem. When I harvest, I try to only take 10% to 25% of each type of plant I collect. This ensures that the plant I am taking will not be harmed in the process. In addition, some plants really like to be cut, but only a small amount, so this rule helps me make sure that the plant will have a healthy portion of its leaves cut off.

A Strong Ecological Connection:

Humans have always had a very strong connection to nature. Wild harvesting carries this connection further, helping to strengthen your local ecosystems. For example, when you snip and pluck a few leaves off of your local edible plants, it simulates wild animals eating leaves, which promotes future strong growth. In addition, wild harvesting can be very beneficial ecologically, especially if you are harvesting plants which otherwise would take needless time, energy, money, and resources to purchase.

Furthering the Spread of Plants:

Lastly in the topic of wild harvesting, you can take it upon yourself to try and spread plants further, in order to strengthen and grow your local ecosystems. To do this, you want to take a few seed pods (or fresh seeds) when the plants are ready and spread them further, but to neighboring areas. This can strengthen the ecosystem by adding plants that can house/feed animals, and promote pollination by local bees and insects.

A Final takeaway:

In the end, growing and harvesting tea is a very rewarding process, and can help with a variety of illnesses. You should always work within your means during this process, as to not stress yourself out too much. And always, you should remember that this process is purely a hobby and you should above everything else have fun!